Bubbles

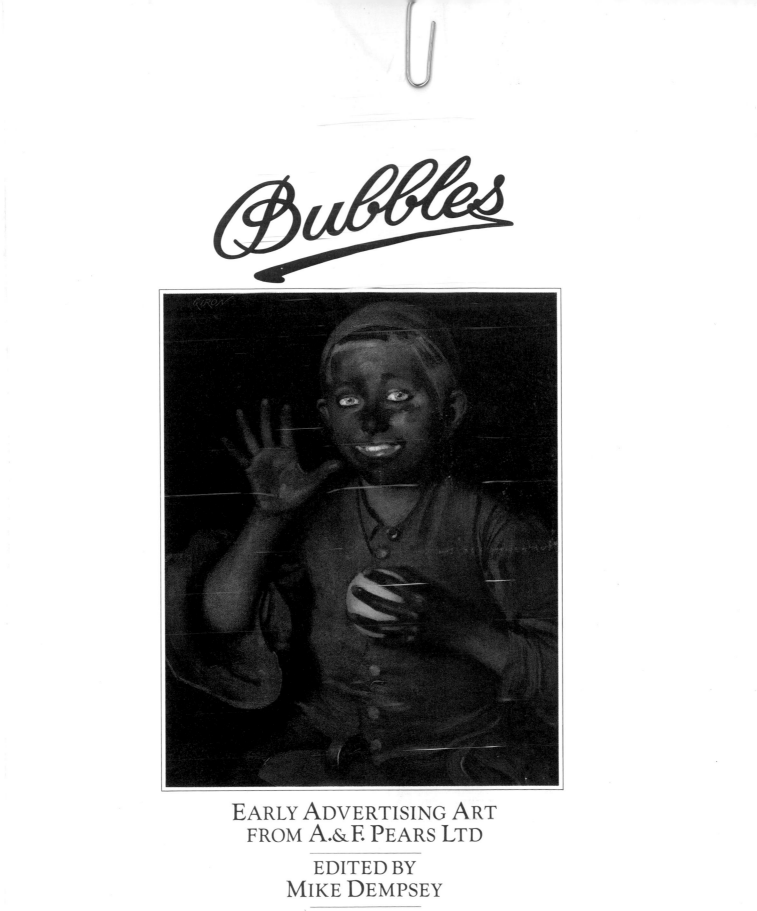

Early Advertising Art
from A. & F. Pears Ltd

EDITED BY
MIKE DEMPSEY

WITH AN INTRODUCTION BY
TIM SHACKLETON

FONTANA PAPERBACKS

First published in Fontana Paperbacks 1978
The text and arrangement of this collection
are copyright
© Wm. Collins Sons & Co. Ltd. 1978
12345678910

Pears' Soap.   Pears' Soap.

For Polly, Joe and Ben

The publishers gratefully acknowledge the assistance
of A. & F. Pears Ltd, and in particular Mr Tony
Wyer, in the preparation of this book, and
the Museum of London for permission to
reproduce 'The Bayswater Omnibus' by
George William Joy.

Because a small number of the printed originals
used in this book were not in perfect condition,
they have been trimmed slightly to mask off
damaged areas.

Made and printed in Great Britain by
William Collins Sons & Co. Ltd., Glasgow

The enviable international reputation and commercial success which the London-based firm of A. & F. Pears has enjoyed for nearly two hundred years is due largely to the efforts of two men: Andrew Pears, a farmer's son from Cornwall, and Thomas J. Barratt, a man often referred to as the father of modern advertising. Between them, though a generation was to separate their individual involvement with the firm, they evolved a classic threefold formula for success: spotting a gap on the market, developing a high-quality product to fill it, and convincing as many people as possible to buy that product by the use of extensive promotion and advertising.

Andrew Pears arrived in London in 1789 from his native Cornish village of Mevagissey, where he had trained as a barber. He opened premises in Gerrard Street, Soho – then a fashionable residential area – and was soon enjoying considerable patronage from wealthy families, whose tonsorial needs were attended to by Pears in their own homes. The Gerrard Street shop was used for the manufacture and sale of rouges, powders, creams, dentifrices and other beauty aids – preparations used extensively by the rich to cover up the damage caused by the harsh soaps then used in Britain. The astute Cornishman recognised the potential of a purer, more gentle soap which would treat more kindly the delicate alabaster complexions then in favour (the upper classes unfavourably associated tanned faces with those of the lower orders who were obliged to toil out of doors for a living). He set about perfecting a manufacturing process for such a product and after much trial and error hit upon a method – which remains substantially similar even today – involving removing impurities and refining the base soap before adding the delicate perfume of English garden flowers. Not only was this product of high quality, it also possessed the great novelty value of being transparent. And it was this latter aspect which gave Pears Soap just the image it needed to be clearly identified by the public.

Though other products were manufactured alongside the transparent soap for many, many years (examples can be found in the following pages), it was clear almost from the very start that Andrew Pears' fortune would be vested in his shilling and half-crown squares of amber soap. In 1835 he took on a partner, his grandson Francis Pears, and they moved to new premises at 55 Wells Street, just off the busy shopping thoroughfare of Oxford Street. The business had consolidated to such an extent that three years later old Andrew was able to retire, leaving Francis in sole charge.

Andrew Pears' legacy was a solid, if not particularly extensive or go-ahead trading concern. Like many Victorian small businesses, it catered to a particular class of customer, whom it respected and wished to please. Andrew Pears was a cautious man, and he cared more for the quality of the products that bore his name than the number of people who bought them. Dogged by inferior imitations, at one stage he even went so far as to sign personally every package he sold. Because of the high price of his products, the market for them was necessarily an exclusive one, and there was little need or point in extensive advertising to try and widen this. Expenditure on sales promotion in the early Victorian period rarely exceeded £80 per annum.

Sensing the impending stagnation of the firm, and recognising the increasing buying power of the middle classes, Francis Pears realised that unless he developed and expanded the family firm he would soon be pushed to one side by more competitive rivals. New offices were opened in Great Russell Street, Bloomsbury, and in 1862 he bought a house and land at Isleworth in Middlesex, where he built a factory which he placed under the dominion of his young son Andrew. Widespread changes soon took place in the sedate and gentlemanly atmosphere of the West End offices, and into the firm came

THOMAS J. BARRATT (1842-1914)

a new partner, Thomas J. Barratt, who had married Francis Pears' eldest daughter Mary. Barratt was far-sighted, aggressive, willing to take risks and infinitely resourceful. Within months he had completely revolutionised Pears' distribution system and was turning his hand towards improving the firm's sales performance by means of expensive and highly original publicity schemes. All this was too much even for Francis Pears, who, fearing imminent bankruptcy, withdrew from the firm, taking most of the money and leaving only £4000 as a loan to be discharged equally by his son and Barratt, who were to remain in sole charge of the business.

Barratt has many modern counterparts in the advertising agencies of Madison Avenue, and his methods were to become widely followed. He imported a quarter of a million French ten-centime pieces (accepted in lieu of a penny in Britain), had the name 'Pears' stamped on every one of them and put the coins into circulation. Since there was no law forbidding the defacing of foreign currency, his scheme earned Pears much valuable publicity until an Act of Parliament could be hastily introduced to declare all foreign coinage illegal tender. The offending coins were withdrawn from circulation and melted down. He persuaded prominent skin specialists, doctors and chemists to give glowing testimonials to Pears Soap; among these were Sir Erasmus Wilson, President of the Royal College of Surgeons, and Doctor Redwood, Professor of Chemistry and Pharmacy to the Pharmaceutical Society of Great Britain, who personally guaranteed that Pears Soap possessed 'the properties of an efficient yet mild detergent without any of the objectionable properties of ordinary soaps'. Such endorsements were boldly displayed in magazine and newspaper advertisements, as handbills and on posters. Lillie Langtry, a highly popular actress of the day, cheerfully gave Barratt a commendation for Pears Soap (for which, as with the other illustrious patrons, no fee was asked) and he broke into the American market by persuading the enormously influential religious leader Henry Ward Beecher to equate cleanliness, and Pears Soap in particular, with Godliness – Barratt promptly buying up the whole of the front page of the *New York Herald* on which to display this glowing testimonial. It seemed no stone was left unturned in Barratt's endless search for good publicity. Infants whose arrival in the world was commemorated in the columns of *The Times* received a complimentary cake of soap and pictorial advertising leaflets by courtesy of Barratt. His most audacious publicity scheme, which in the end failed to get off the ground, was an offer of £100,000 to the British Government to buy the back page of a contemporary national census form for Pears' use. Had he succeeded, Barratt would have put his firm's name before 35,000,000 people's eyes.

But the best-remembered piece of publicity which Barratt devised was the use of Sir John Everett Millais' painting 'Bubbles' as an advertisement for Pears. The model for 'Bubbles' was the

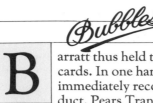

artist's grandson, Willie (later Admiral Sir William) James, and the curly-headed little boy made his first appearance at the Grosvenor Gallery in London in 1886; the picture was originally titled 'A Child's World'. The picture was bought by Sir William Ingram of the *Illustrated London News* for reproduction as a presentation plate in that magazine, and after use it was sold to Barratt for £2200. Though this gave Pears exclusive copyright on the picture, Millais' permission had still to be obtained before it could be modified (by the addition of a bar of transparent soap) for use as an advertisement. At first Millais, then unquestionably the richest and most popular

PEARS' HEADQUARTERS DURING THE BARRATT ERA AT 71-75 NEW OXFORD ST.

painter in Britain, was apprehensive about such pointedly commercial exploitation of his work, but mollified by the high quality of the proofs which Barratt brought to his studio, he gradually warmed to the idea. Once the advertisement appeared he was obliged to defend himself vigorously against a hostile art world, and even as late as 1899, three years after his death, the affair was still a matter for debate in letters to *The Times*.

Barratt claimed to have spent £30,000 on the 'Bubbles' campaign, and the number of individual reproductions of the painting ran into millions. By any standards, it was an unqualified success, whatever the critics had to say. Even today, 'Bubbles' remains one of the most instantly recognisable advertising symbols ever devised, and many of the prints which Pears later made available to the public were framed and hung in living rooms around the world. Barratt evidently had a ready eye for the commercial potential of art, for another of his acquisitions, Landseer's 'Monarch of the Glen', though never used by Pears themselves beyond appearing as a colour plate in the 1916 *Pears Annual*, duly became the distinctive trademark of the distilling firm of John Dewar & Sons, with whom A. & F. Pears had links.

Barratt thus held two trump cards. In one hand was an immediately recognisable product, Pears Transparent Soap. In the other was the association (in the popular mind at least) between that product and culture, represented by 'Bubbles'. It was a combination which was to represent Pears' public image for many years to come, and continues today with the tradition of each young Miss Pears (the winner of an annual competition) having her portrait painted by a recognised artist. Barratt time and again capitalised on this association. He brought art to the public eye through *Pears Annual*, first published in 1891 and surviving until 1920. The *Annual* was a large-format, limp-cover publication containing, in addition to advertising for Pears' and other firms' products, quality fiction (Dickens's Christmas Books were reprinted in early editions), illustrations (as the years went by there was an increase in the use of colour plates and second-colour tints) and at least two large, separately packaged prints for framing. All this, at least until 1915, for sixpence!

Barratt evidently had philanthropic as well as commercial motives in bringing art to the public eye: the 1897 edition claimed that

'It is beyond controversy that, before the popular advent of *Pears Annual*, pictures of the refined quality of our Presentation Plates (which surpass any works of even this high-class order ever previously attempted) were unattainable by picture-lovers at anything less than a guinea a-piece.

'Our ambition has been to offer an appreciative and increasing public, which has grown to expect these advantages at our hands, presentation pictures of superior quality and of artistic values, to ensure our extended popularity, and to constitute *Pears Annual* the foremost achievement of this kind . . .

'The *bonne bouche* of *Pears Annual* 1897 will be readily recognised in the two large Presentation Plates, after the late and ever-to-be-lamented President of the Royal Academy, Sir John Everett Millais, whose two *chefs-d'oeuvre*, the well-known pictures, 'Cherry Ripe' and 'Bubbles', are now placed within the means of the million for the first time, so beautifully reproduced as scarcely to be distinguishable from the original pictures themselves . . . which now have a value of more than £10,000 the pair. And whilst so long as *Pears Annual* is produced it will ever be our aim, so far as it is in our power, to maintain its excellence, we do not expect again to have the opportunity of furnishing you with such a pair of pictures as these – worthy, as they are, of being framed and hung in the first and most artistic houses in the land.'

Two points in this lurching piece of Victorian prose are worth picking up on. Firstly, the chromolithographic plates were undoubtedly 'beautifully reproduced', since they were printed from no less than 24 separate colour blocks; this book, as with almost all modern book production, uses a mere four impositions. Secondly, they were 'scarcely to be distinguishable from the original pictures' through a painstaking

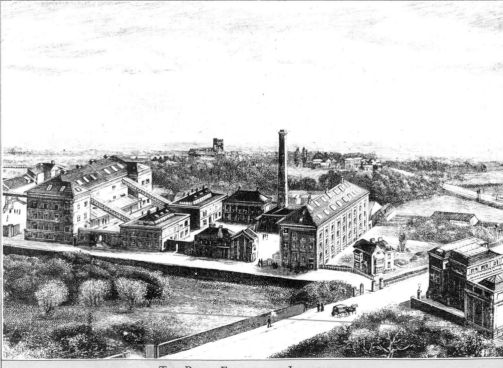

THE PEARS FACTORY AT ISLEWORTH.

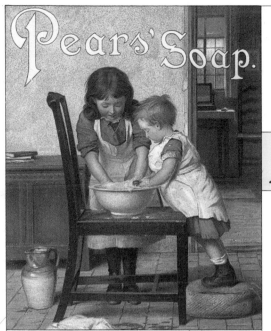

process (made defunct by the advent of photolithography) in which the original painting was copied and etched out by craftsmen on to each of the 24 stone blocks in turn. The original artists for these presentation plates included Frank Dadd, J. C. Dollman, Hugh Thompson, Will Owen (of 'Bisto Kids' fame), Maurice Greiffenhagen, Gordon Browne and Tom Browne. They were printed in huge quantities; records survive showing that Pears spent £17,500 on producing the 'Bubbles' print alone and almost all were still available to order by the time the last issue of *Pears Annual* appeared in 1920. Coloured frontispieces, which generally repeated material used in the *Annual* or as ad-advertisements, were also used in the famous *Pears Cyclopaedia*, first published in 1897 and still issued today.

Barratt died on 28 April 1914, aged 72. He was widely mourned, particularly among the press and advertising fraternities. To the latter especially he had opened up new horizons; he joined Pears at a time when advertising was limited by and large to small newspaper advertisements and crudely executed handbills and posters, and lived to see it brought, to a great extent through his own example, to undreamt-of sophistication. He forced the manufacturing world to see the advantages of paying good money for good advertising; in the 1880s Pears were spending between £30,000 and £40,000 a year on advertising and by 1907 the figure had risen to £126,000. He pioneered the technique, so familar today, of saturation advertising; W. E. Gladstone, searching for a metaphor to convey a sense of vast quantity during a debate on a topic now forgotten in the House of Commons,

suggested the articles in question were 'as numerous as the advertisements of Pears Soap, or as autumn leaves in Vallombrosa'. On hoardings and on railway stations, in the press and on buses, the name of Pears Soap was everywhere in Victorian and Edwardian times.

And what of the material which Barratt put before the public, and which is reproduced in this book? Much of it strikes the modern eye as unashamedly sentimental, but this was to the taste of the day – a taste which Pears were quick to recognise and cater for. Children (whether angelic or recalcitrant), animals, flowers and beautiful women are common denominators in the market appeal of advertising, especially when aimed, as Pears Soap mostly was, at female buyers. Pears' slogans – 'Matchless for the complexion', 'Good morning! Have you used Pears Soap?' – were simple and unchanging, reflecting an era of guilelessness and security in which the good things in life might reasonably be taken for granted – at least by the more fortunate. Only the pictures themselves changed from time to time, and it is interesting to look at a 1907 newspaper interview with Barratt in which he says

'Tastes change, fashions change, and the advertiser has to change with them. An idea that was effective a generation ago would fall flat, stale, and unprofitable if presented to the public today. Not that the idea of to-day is always better than the older idea, but it is different – it hits the present taste.'

A generation! Modern advertising

thinks in terms of weeks, its campaigns changing direction like yachts in a strong breeze.

Pears advertising, to suit its brand image, was tasteful and restrained, needing no recourse to the hyperbolics often encountered elsewhere in the period we are considering. The message was simple: that Pears Soap was safe and healthy and that it made its users beautiful. It savours of prestige advertising, embodying an unquestioned market supremacy; probably there is a good hint of snobbery here as well, for while the middle classes are invariably seen as healthy and self-assured, their social inferiors like servants, ragged urchins and in particular black people are frequently seen as figures of fun. In design terms, many of the advertisements illustrated here could be stripped of their typography and considered purely as genre paintings – as some of them indeed originally were. Though the product name and captions are generally in harmony with the pictures, they are typical of this transitional period of advertising design in that lettering and illustration are not considered as a single unified and integrated entity. But their appeal is simple and immediate, requiring no sophisticated interpretation: they provoke an emotional rather than intellectual response. Barratt aimed, he said, to make his advertisements 'telling, artistic, picturesque, attractive, pretty, amusing' – and of course commercially successful. If for nothing more than that they took art out of the galleries and into homes and streets, thus brightening the humdrum lives of ordinary people, they are worthy of remembrance.

'THE INVADERS' BY ARTHUR J. ELSLEY, A PRESENTATION PLATE WITH THE 1915 PEARS ANNUAL.

Opposite Probably the most
famous curly-headed kid ever.
'Bubbles' was painted by Sir
John Everett Millais in 1886 and
later bought by Thomas Barratt
for exclusive use in promoting
Pears Soap. **Below** Bathtime for
baby: an engraved handbill of
1886.

Opposite Looking more like
torture than a close shave, this
advertisement promoting Pears'
shilling shaving sticks appeared
in 1891. **Below** The cover of a
small booklet on hygiene
produced in 1887.

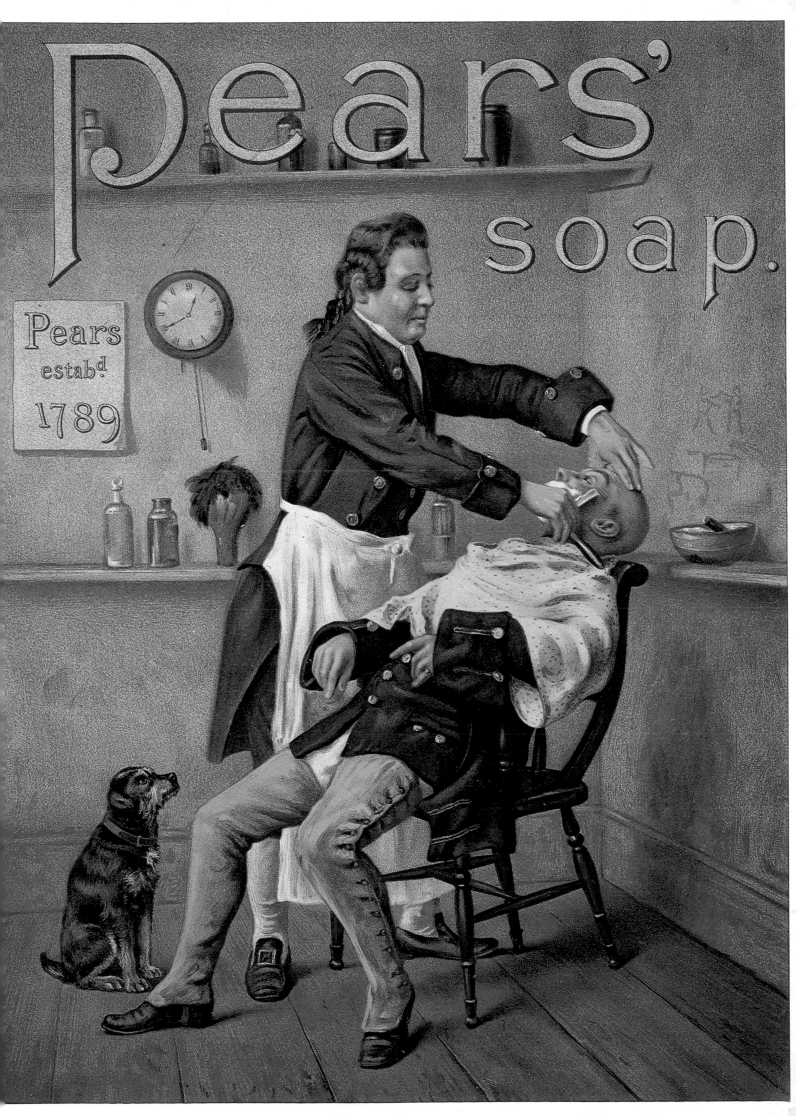

Bubbles

Opposite Gently flying through the air on a lazy summer's day: 'After School' by Fred Morgan, a presentation print with the Christmas 1893 *Pears Annual*. **Below** Even mums in Japan were using it! Or so this handbill, first used in 1887, would have us believe.

Opposite A rather surreal
advertisement of 1892 depicting
some old familiar faces used in
singing the praises of the
transparent wonder. Below
Forcefully endorsing her views,
Mrs Lillie Langtry appeared in
a popular advertisement of
1889.

Opposite A bracing stroll along
the sands with friends. This
presentation print, 'Sea Horses'
by Fred Morgan, appeared in
1894. Note the subtle 'Pears'
drawn in the sand. **Below**
Hail Pears! A handbill of 1887.

Opposite It's marvellous what a little soap can do: this old gent appeared in 1893 and was used, like many Pears advertisements, both on posters and in the press. **Below** 'The Formula of British Conquest', an outrageous press advertisement from 1891.

THE FORMULA OF BRITISH CONQUEST

PEARS SOAP IS THE BEST

REG^D COPYRIGHT

PEARS' SOAP IN THE SOUDAN.

" Even if our invasion of the Soudan has done nothing else it has at any rate left the Arab something to puzzle his fuzzy head over, for the legend
PEARS' SOAP IS THE BEST,
inscribed in huge white characters on the rock which marks the farthest point of our advance towards Berber, will tax all the wits of the Dervishes of the Desert to translate."—Phil Robinson, *War Correspondent (in the Soudan) of the Daily Telegraph in London*, 1884.

Opposite A fine example of
sentimental schmaltz that even
Norman Rockwell would have
been proud of. Titled
'Suspense' and painted by
Burton Barber, it was given
away with *Pears Annual* in 1895.
Below This advertisement was
the subject of a delightful
send-up in 'Punch', 1884
(see page 48).

PEARS' SOAP

Mrs. LANGTRY says—

Since using **PEARS' SOAP** *for
the hands and complexion I have discarded
all others.*

Lillie Langtry

Opposite This poor little
blighter has a heavy burden to
carry but still manages to
deliver Pears' Christmas
greetings for 1894.
Below A nice piece of fantasy
in this simple message of 1887.

A SPECIALTY FOR INFANTS.

Opposite Millais' rosy-cheeked
sweetie 'Cherry Ripe' was,
along with 'Bubbles', given
away as a presentation print
with the 1897 *Annual*. **Below**
This sultry beauty graced the
pages of the *Graphic* in 1886.

Opposite Maynard Brown's
superbly vibrant cover for
the 1897 *Pears Annual*, bearing
a heavy French stylistic
influence.
Below Well have you? The
ultimate 'hand' bill, 1888.

Pears' Annual

1897

A MERRY XMAS TO YOU

CONTENTS.

The whole Printed in England.

The unmistakable style of
Charles Robinson. These two
photolithographic illustrations
were part of four, titled 'The
Seasons', especially
commissioned to be given
away free with the *Annual* in
1920. **Below** 'Spring'. **Opposite**
'Summer'.

Opposite A seductive glance
from the 1898 *Pears Annual*
cover. Below Society beauties
need to start caring for their
complexions at a tender age:
a press advertisement from an
1895 *Illustrated London News*.

PEARS' SOAP

·a·Specialty·for·Children·

Pears' Annual

1898

A MERRY XMAS TO YOU

Opposite Poised for action, the 'Captain of the Eleven' was painted by P. H. Calderon. A very popular presentation print was produced in 1889.
Below Henry Stacy Marks produced many engravings for Pears. This one was entitled 'The Birth of Civilization' and appeared as a handbill in 1890.

Pears

Opposite Here's looking at
you, kid! The delightful cover
for *Pears' Annual*, 1899. **Below**
'The Bayswater Omnibus',
1895, by George William Joy
shows two Pears' posters –
'Lillie Langtry' and 'Bubbles'
– in everyday use.

Pears'

CHRISTMAS 1899

ANNUAL

A MERRY XMAS TO YOU

Opposite A welcome break for
Pears from childhood scenes,
this beautiful print of petunias
and geraniums by one Miss
Mutrie, titled 'Summer Glory',
was presented with the 1899
Annual. **Below** This poor little
sweep about to be collared and
scrubbed clean appeared in
1892.

Opposite and **below** Babies in
abundance; these two cheeky
monkeys delighted mums as
advertisements in 1899.

PEARS' SOAP IS THE BEST.

Pears' Soap

"Impudence"

Opposite One in the eye: a
poster by Phil May from 1900
shows how a Pears' beauty
disturbed this barber's
concentration. Below A
bill-poster breaking the law
in 1895.

Opposite A guilty smile before
the thrashing. These naughty
companions graced the pages
of *Pears Annual*, 1900. Below
The shaving stick that lasted a
year and cost only a shilling.
A handbill of 1895.

PEARS' SOAP.—The Shaver's Delight.

Opposite One to think about:
this nice piece of understatement
appeared in 1903.
Below 'The Dirty Boy'
started out in life as a sculpture
by Focadi and was bought by
Thomas Barratt for use in a
very successful campaign.

Opposite This child is in for a
very rough time, much to the
enjoyment of the onlookers.
Below Another Henry Stacy
Marks handbill which appeared
in 1898, shortly after his death.

Bubbles

Opposite More *Watership
Down* than *Alice in Wonderland*,
Fred Morgan's presentation
print appeared in the 1904
Pears Annual. **Below** One of
Phil May's last works for Pears.

**A Humorous Pears' Soap Advertisement
drawn by the late PHIL MAY.**

Opposite Look! it's transparent!
A perfect little darling tiptoes
off to bed; an advertisement of
1902. **Below** This famous
send-up by Harry Furniss of
Lillie Langtry's testimonial was
put to good use by Thomas
Barratt. It first appeared in the
pages of *Punch* on 26 April,
1884.

Opposite 'The Snowball—Guilty
or Not Guilty' by H. Piffard
has a delightful tension between
the two figures. **Below** 'More
Bubbles' was produced as a
print to complement Millais'
more famous creation.

Opposite Behind those pretty
eyes lurks a mischievous little
creature. Cover of *Pears Annual*,
1907. **Below** All grown up and
able to wash himself, this little
lad was used in periodicals
in 1909.

Pears' Annual
1907

6D

complete with 4 coloured presentation

Opposite A distinctly strange looking dog enjoys 'A Quiet Pipe'. He was painted by Sir Edwin Landseer, whose more famous painting, 'The Monarch of the Glen', was also owned by Thomas Barratt before going to graze with John Dewar & Sons. **Below** An advertisement by Walter Crane from 1911.

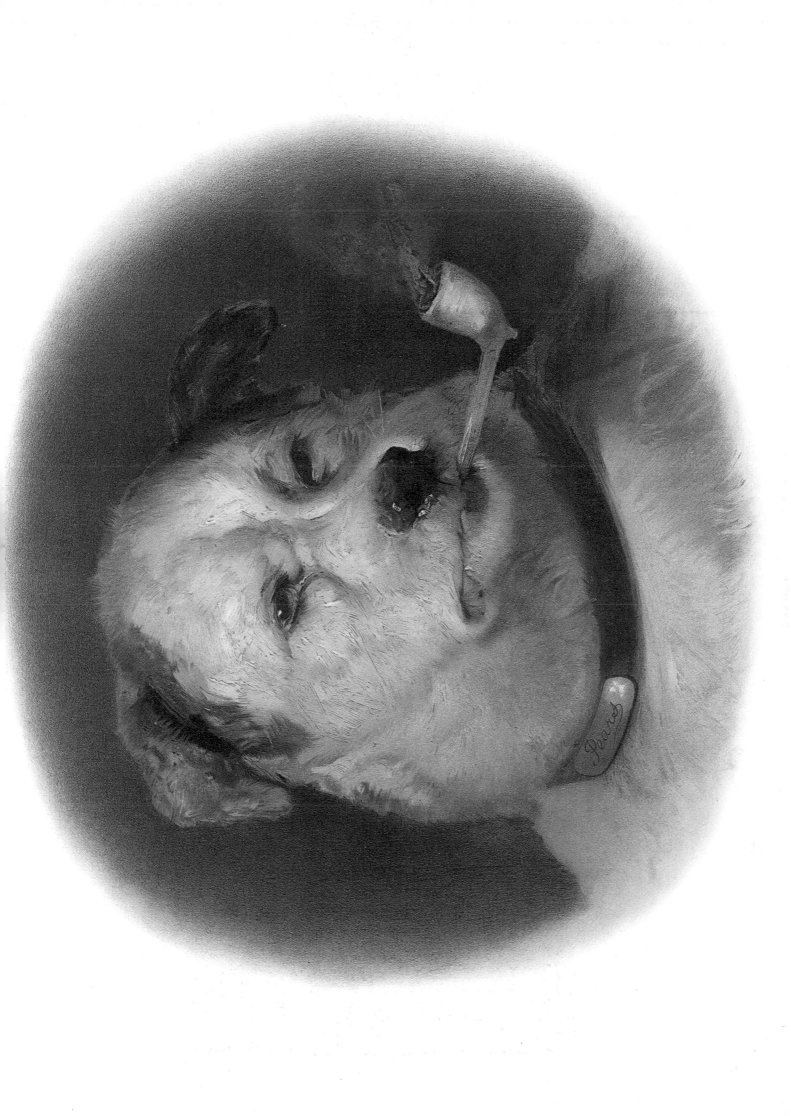

Opposite The traditional
Christmas scene 'Waiting for
the Coach' graced the cover of
the 1911 *Annual*. Below An
unusual advertisement by
Henry Stacy Marks; why
should monks care particularly
about delicate complexions?

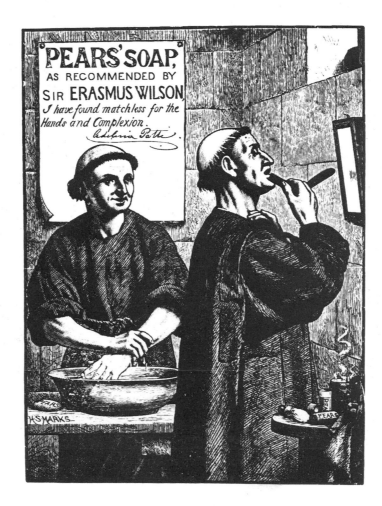

PEARS' ANNUAL
Christmas 1911

Bubbles

Opposite This highly intelligent
dog, no doubt reading *Pears
Cyclopaedia*, was painted by
Briton Riviere. Entitled
'Naughty Boy or Compulsory
Education' it was produced as
a presentation print in 1909.
Below One of the many
multi-endorsed advertisements
that appeared in magazines all
over the United States.

Opposite Cleanliness is next to
Godliness, or so it seems in
this advertisement of 1910.
Below One of many games and
puzzles to amuse readers of
Pears Annual.

A CONUNDRUM.

Question :

What is the difference between

and

an Arab Steed ?

Answer :

One washes

the Beautiful, and the other

Scours the Plain.

Bubbles

Opposite These two little
sweethearts appeared in a
presentation plate of 1910 by
Fred Morgan entitled 'Over the
Garden Wall'. **Below** A gentle
reminder that war raged on
through 1917.

Opposite This advertisement
of 1915 was titled 'His Turn
Next'. **Below** 'Playmates' by
E. Munier was a presentation
print for 1903.

Opposite Fluffy bunnies
contrast with the peaches-and-
cream complexions of these
two little railway children,
painted by G. Sheridan Knowles
for *Pears' Annual* in 1913. Note
Barratt's initials on the trunk and
basket. **Below** Getting to grips with
the snow: 'Pluck' painted by
Maynard Brown as a
presentation print for
Christmas 1892.

Opposite 'Autumn' and **below**
'Winter' by Charles Robinson
were from a set of four prints
called 'The Seasons'
commissioned for the 1920
Annual.

Opposite Eighty years on from
'Bubbles' Peter Blake, father of
the Brotherhood of Ruralists,
carries on the tradition of
Pears children's portraits.
Below One of the many uses
that 'Bubbles' was put to:
personal postcards at 6d. a
dozen with an addition not in
the original on page 7. Guess
what it is.

"BUBBLES."
By Sir John Millais, Bt., P.R.A.
After the Original in the possession of Messrs. Pears

The Sweetest
PICTURE POST CARD
Yet Produced.

As Beautiful as a fine miniature painting and
a picture everyone will prize.

"BUBBLES,"

By SIR JOHN E. MILLAIS, Bart.,
President of the Royal Academy.

A Neat Packet
containing
One Dozen.

POST **6**d. FREE.

SEND POSTAL ORDER OR STAMPS.

Published by A. & F. PEARS, Ltd.,
71-75, New Oxford St., LONDON, W.C.

Please mark the top left-hand corner of
your envelope with the word "NEAT."

Design & Art Direction, Mike Dempsey/Editorial Direction, Tim Shackleton/Colour separations, Gilchrist Bros, Leeds